YOU EARNED IT. NOW KEEP IT!
A COMMON SENSE GUIDE TO SENIOR PLANNING

by Donald H. Chapin, Esq.

Certified as an Elder Law Attorney by the
National Elder Law Foundation

Chapin Law Offices
Practice Limited to Elder Law

www.chapinlawoffices.com

Chapin Law Offices
Copyright © 2003

© 2003 Donald H. Chapin.
Printed and bound in the United States of America.

Notice of Rights

All rights reserved. No part of this book may be reproduced or transmitted in any form or by any means, electronic or mechanical, including photocopying, recording, or by any information storage or retrieval system – except by a reviewer who may quote brief passages in a review to be printed in a magazine, newspaper or on the Web – without permission in writing from the publisher. For more information contact: Don H. Chapin at www.chapinlawoffices.com.

Notice of Liability

Although the author and publisher have made every effort to ensure the accuracy and completeness of information contained in this book, we assume no responsibility for errors, inaccuracies, omissions, or any inconsistency herein. Any slight of people, places, or organizations are unintentional.

First printing 2003
Second printing 2005
Third printing 2005

ISBN 0-9728103-0-7

CONTENTS

Forward
by Tom McNutt..2

Introduction..4

The Seven Step Process..7

Chapter 1
Step 1: Gain Knowledge..10

Chapter 2
Step 2: Personal Commitment..13

Chapter 3
Step 3: Dream..15

Chapter 4
Step 4: Eliminate Needless Taxes..................................17

Chapter 5
Step 5: Choose No Probate..27

Chapter 6
Step 6: Stop Nursing Home Spend-Down......................34

Chapter 7
Step 7: Regular Review..47

Chapter 8
Small Business..49

Definition of Terms..53

FOREWORD

Are the golden years behind us or still ahead? While none of us knows what the future holds, we all would like to think that we have many golden years ahead. But if something happens to you today, will your assets be protected and preserved for tomorrow?

When I retired from The Ohio State University in 1988, my wife and I thought our estate plan was complete and final. However, health conditions, special needs, and law changes have caused us to take a critical look at our plan. And that's what this book will help you to do.

As I read the draft for this book, I was intrigued with the common sense approach to such a complex problem. Conventional wisdom has called for tinkering with the approach to estate planning. We need to think "outside the box," and gain knowledge about law changes. We need to dream and continue setting goals. How can we eliminate needless taxes, preserve assets, and still take care of our personal commitments?

This book's highlight lies in the meticulous care taken to provide very specific information on how to develop a plan to preserve what we have so diligently worked for during our lives.

Seniors have waited a long time, perhaps a lifetime, for a text of high quality and accuracy on the subject of estate planning that helps to protect and preserve their assets. Elder Law Attorney Don H. Chapin has given us the tools with this book. It is, indeed, common sense for the golden years.

Tom McNutt

Professor Emeritus,
The Ohio State University

Garden Expert, NBC4 TV

INTRODUCTION

I wrote this *Common Sense Guide* to give Ohio seniors a comprehensive resource as they prepare an estate plan to protect and preserve their assets. The information in this guide is current as of 2002. Since laws do change, seniors can use this information as a tool in their planning, but it is imperative that they consult a trusted elder law attorney who will clarify current laws.

Today's seniors are trusting by nature. They grew up in a time when a person's word became his unwavering promise. Today if they are offered advice from an "authority," most seniors expect the advice to be truthful. Unfortunately, there are many uncaring and unscrupulous people whose "advice" turns out to be either worthless or misleading. Our state and local governments also provide advice to seniors. Unfortunately again, this advice usually benefits government more than seniors. For these and other reasons, seniors sometimes suffer catastrophic financial losses.

That's why this guide exists. It allows seniors to develop their own approach to planning for retirement that goes well beyond ordinary financial planning. The *Common Sense Guide* makes it possible for seniors and their adult children to understand and make decisions about sophisticated elder law and estate distribution issues. Many families have been crushed by financial disaster because of confusing government regulations, lack of accurate information, and misleading or bad advice from self-proclaimed "investment advisors."

Almost all of us know a family in which the husband or wife is stricken with a serious illness like Alzheimer's disease or dementia. After family members come to terms with the diagnosis, they may be overwhelmed with the onslaught of information and misinformation. Misinformation can lead to financial disaster, especially if a nursing home stay is involved.

Your best protection is to seek a financial advisor who knows the details of elder law. Unfortunately, many financial advisors play the role of legal advisor as well. Even if their advice is well intentioned, financial advisors can never know the details of elder law unless they specialize in elder law. Don't rely on the legal advice of your financial advisor just because you are comfortable with him or her or because you don't trust lawyers. Find an elder law attorney to complement the advice from your financial advisor.

The world can be hazardous to your assets. There are laws in place that can set up a chain of events leading to financial ruin for families. Seniors cannot trust that laws, government officials, health care administrators, and investment advisors are working for their best interest. Seniors must protect their own assets.

During my time practicing elder law, I have found that just a little bit of planning and foresight can make it possible for families to take back control of events in their lives and prevent the government (and often our legal system) from draining a lifetime of work and savings. With the same small amount of planning, seniors can avoid being misled by demanding health care administrators or "quick fix" investment counselors.

The purpose of this *Common Sense Guide* is to focus on controlling several key issues:

- How to make transfers to heirs during your life to minimize taxes

- How to benefit from charitable giving

- How to make sure your heirs (not the government) receive your wealth

- How to preserve assets from nursing home spend-down

- How to avoid probate fees

- How to settle an estate privately

- How to preserve assets from lawsuits and creditors

Dealing with these issues requires a planning process like the one I developed.

The Seven Step Process

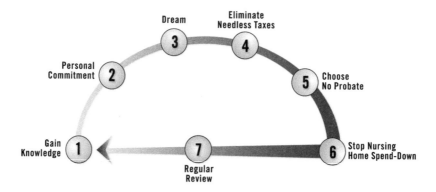

1. **Gain Knowledge** – Good and accurate information is necessary for making informed decisions for family estate planning. Seniors must understand the laws and regulations that will affect their future income, their ability to retire comfortably, and their capability to leave a legacy to their family and loved ones.

2. **Personal Commitment** – Talking about planning is easy. Actually doing something means making a commitment. How do you get to that point?

3. **Dream** – Most times our capacity to dream results from life experiences. Dreaming means setting life goals. Just because you're retired doesn't mean you stop setting goals.

4. **Eliminate Needless Taxes** – With the proper planning, income taxes on retirement income can be minimized, and capital gains taxes, estate taxes, gift taxes, and recovery taxes can be reduced or avoided.

5. **Choose No Probate** – How can you avoid this antiquated legal process that causes unnecessary delay and needless drain of money for many families who are quite capable of handling their own affairs?

6. **Stop Nursing Home Spend-Down** – What does Medicare pay and what doesn't it pay? It's important to understand how to ensure your loved one receives the care needed and doesn't lose self-esteem. What rights do patients and families have?

7. **Regular Review** – Family relationships evolve, health conditions change, life goals change, and laws change. A plan must be reviewed regularly to ensure it meets the family's current needs.

While there are many well-meaning people serving seniors and many well-intentioned attorneys advising them, laws and regulations are so complicated and complex that even advice given with the best of intentions can get families into financial trouble. It is imperative that seniors and their families work with individuals who are licensed to practice elder law, are knowledgeable, and who handle these matters on a daily basis. Check credentials and references, and make sure you have complete faith and trust in your advisor.

Don H. Chapin, *Certified Elder Law Attorney*

Certified as an Elder Law Attorney by the
National Elder Law Foundation

CHAPTER I

∾

Step 1
GAIN KNOWLEDGE

There are a number of different ways to approach each individual family's situation. If you take control of your family assets, you can minimize taxes, significantly reduce legal fees and administrative charges, prevent squandering of your investments and savings to pay expenses, and even deter needless nursing home spend-down.

YOU EARNED IT.

Find an elder law attorney you trust and begin asking questions. Discuss your current financial situation and where you want to be in the next five, 10, or 15 years. Consider your assets and how you want to pass them to your heirs (tax free, of course).

It's also important to consider future health care costs. Although Americans pay into Medicare all their lives to ensure health care coverage during retirement, Medicare has not kept pace with seniors' medical needs. Unfortunately, Medicare discriminates against some people because it does not always cover illnesses like Parkinson's disease, Alzheimer's disease, Amyotrophic Lateral Sclerosis (ALS), or stroke rehabilitation. In other words, Medicare pays for some medical conditions but not others, despite the fact that people pay into Medicare all of their working lives.

The AARP recently released a study showing that Medicare covers only 6 to 8% of nursing home costs. If Medicare doesn't cover it, then your Medicare supplement usually will not cover those costs either. Unfortunately, many financial planners don't bother to discuss future health care costs with their clients. Instead, many suggest long-term care insurance as a quick and easy fix. It's not a quick and easy fix at all.

Gaining knowledge before beginning the planning process is priceless. Consider the following: A 79-year-old woman came to see me with a briefcase full of papers. She was responsible for the family business after her husband's death. His love was farming, and he had

11

not considered an estate plan. When she sat down, she began with this haunting statement, "I know I have a problem, but I don't know where to look!"

Together we sorted through the various documents and discovered her problem: the federal "death" tax. Although her intention was to leave the farm to her three sons, she needed to develop an estate plan to ensure her sons would not have to sell the farm to pay the Federal Estate Tax upon her death. Realizing the degree of the financial penalty if she didn't plan ahead, we quickly put a plan in place that wiped out that liability. There are financial risks in not planning! Retirement can no longer mean disengagement from the world. Seniors need to take charge of their assets. You've worked a lifetime for your retirement and now you need to preserve your assets so you don't outlive your savings.

Success in any endeavor usually means an attitude of continuous learning. Retirement is no exception. Seniors must set goals and learn about estate planning, thereby gaining self-confidence about what legal actions they should take.

CHAPTER 2

༄

Step 2
PERSONAL COMMITMENT

Before making a commitment, it is important to understand the outcomes:

- Financial gain

- Resolution of "sticky" family issues

- Reassurance that your family won't become a victim (because you control the events)

It is important to understand that neither the U.S. Internal Revenue Service (IRS) nor the Ohio Department of Job and Family Services (ODJFS) are committed to saving your money. If you want to save taxes and defeat nursing home spend-down, you must take charge. You are the only one who can be personally committed to the process.

Seniors are not the only ones making a personal commitment to preserve assets. Often an adult child is the one who jump-starts the process. For example, a woman whose mother had died realized her father's most valuable asset was his home. An elder law attorney executed a deed on the house in the daughter's name, allowing her father to retain control of the home. From that day forward, the house was no longer a part of the probate estate. If the daughter had not committed to helping her father with an estate plan before he died, his house would have gone through the probate process, and she may have had to sell it to pay lawyers' fees. Additionally, the house would have been subject to the Ohio Estate Recovery Tax.

CHAPTER 3

༄

Step 3

DREAM

Believe it or not, dreaming is a profoundly important part of making your plans. It is all part of a process to ensure you create a customized, personalized plan. Estate planning is much more than executing a set of documents, or signing up for insurance, or making investments. Your plan should make common sense to you, be flexible for you to live your life, and lead you to your dreams.

Retirement doesn't mean you don't have to plan. Set a direction for your family. If you allow someone else to set a direction for you, how will you achieve your dreams? Choose a time period – one, three, or five years. Decide where you want to be and ask your advisor how to get there.

Dreaming and planning can be easy. Begin by following this simple process:

1. Take a sheet of paper and draw a line down the middle, lengthwise.

2. To the left of the line, write down your assets (insurance policies, real estate, stock options, notes, savings bonds, art, antiques, furniture, vehicles, 401K, IRA, and other retirement funds).

3. To the right of the line, write down your plans for the next five to 10 years.

4. Draw a horizontal line under the two columns. Record how you would like to pass on your assets. Do you want to give away the asset but still control its use? Are there members of your family with special needs for whom you want to ensure quality of life or who need their assets managed for them?

After preparing this one-page planning sheet, discuss the goals with family members you trust and then select advisors to help you. Without doing the "dreaming" part, you won't know if your plan is guiding you down the road you want to take. Don't try to become an expert on planning; just set the direction for your family's estate and future.

∽

16

CHAPTER 4

Step 4
ELIMINATE NEEDLESS TAXES

Avoiding needless taxes is critical to making your plan work. An estate plan must anticipate capital gains taxes, income tax rates from qualified accounts, and both state and federal estate taxes (a.k.a. death taxes). Here are several ways to avoid these taxes.

Gifting

Each U.S. citizen has a personal gift exemption of $1 million. This means you may give away up to $1 million in your lifetime and not pay a gift tax. Some people believe they can only gift $10,000 per year without paying a tax. In 2002, this $10,000 annual exclusion was raised to $11,000.

Every time you give away more than $11,000, it counts against the total $1 million allotted in your lifetime. Each time you give away $11,000 or less, it is not counted against the $1 million. The annual personal exclusion of $11,000 can be gifted with absolutely no paperwork or reporting. Any amount over the annual exemption of $11,000 must be deducted from the $1 million lifetime exemption by filing a gift tax return.

From the gift recipient's point of view, the gift is not taxable income. Whether you receive $1 or $1 million, there is no legal obligation to declare the gift as income for tax purposes. Therefore, many times a gifting strategy can work to lower an estate or keep the appreciation of the asset out of the donor's estate. With the $11,000 rule, it is possible to gift out $110,000 if there are two donors (mother and father) and five children. Absolutely no paperwork needs to be filed even with these large gifts.

YOU EARNED IT.

TO ILLUSTRATE THE GIFTING STRATEGY:

Assets of Mom and Dad	Federal Estate Tax estimated	Ohio Estate Tax estimated
$1,250,000	$125,000	$64,000

If Mom and Dad have five children who are all married and have two children each (10 grandchildren), gifting looks like this:

DAD		MOM	
$11,000 to five children	$55,000	$11,000 to five children	$55,000
$11,000 to five spouses of children	$55,000	$11,000 to five spouses of children	$55,000
$11,000 to ten grandchildren	$110,000	$11,000 to ten grandchildren	$110,000
Total of 20 people	$220,000	Total of 20 people	$220,000

In one year, with no paperwork, the results are as follows:

Gifts of Mom and Dad	Federal Estate Tax estimated	Ohio Estate Tax estimated
$440,000	$0	$33,000*

*ONLY IF DEATH OCCURS 36 MONTHS AFTER THE GIFTS

Therefore, by using this tax-free annual exemption, the tax bill was **lowered $154,000**!

Family Trust

Sometimes people don't like to gift because they lose control. From a psychological point of view, after a lifetime of accumulating assets, people usually don't want to give up their assets voluntarily. However, many families set up Family Irrevocable Trusts and gift assets into these trusts. By using an independent trustee and by naming different beneficiaries, this trust can insulate family assets from the legal problems of divorce or creditors. As long as there is no connection between the grantors and the ability to use and enjoy the assets, either as trustees or as lifetime beneficiaries, creditors cannot get to those assets.

Sometimes the Family Trust is used for residences or farms. However, there are negative consequences of this method:

- Cost basis of the property will pass on to the beneficiaries of the Trust

- If this is a gift, an appraisal and a gift tax return must be filed by the donor

- If a nursing home stay is involved, the gifts are subject to a 60-month look-back period

There is one big benefit to the early gifting of valuable property – any further appreciation is not in the senior's estate.

If a family doesn't want to set up a Family Trust, it might deed the property outright to the children. This has negative consequences from a capital gains tax and nursing home spend-down point of view. If a Family Trust is not desired, a very useful method is a Life Estate Deed.

YOU EARNED IT.

With a Life Estate Deed, a senior deeds the future interest of the property to the children but retains a life or current (present) interest in the property. When the grantor of the deed dies, the grantees will receive full title to the land without probate and with no ongoing capital gains tax liability. In addition, the Life Estate Deed decreases the risk of having to sell the home to move into a nursing home.

Don't be in a hurry to gift real estate. Consider the Family Trust or the Life Estate Deed to determine the best benefits for your family.

Saving Taxes on Retirement Income

Many people have IRAs or other tax-deferred retirement accounts. Even though these IRAs are wonderful for accumulating wealth during your earning years, they can become tax "time bombs" when you retire. All income from these accounts (except the Roth IRA) is taxed as ordinary income.

IRA accounts may be transferred (rolled) to a spouse's IRA without any tax consequences. However, an IRA left to an estate, trust or individual may trigger a higher than desired income tax on the distribution. Therefore, always develop a strategy for withdrawing from the IRA at as low a tax as possible.

Many strategies are available to spread IRA distribution over a life span of children or grandchildren. If this is your goal, then talk with your administration (bank or financial institution) about how to achieve that.

If you have substantial assets in your IRA, it is a prudent strategy to withdraw the money during a 10 to 12-year period after retirement. If you begin withdrawing money in your mid sixties, the IRA will be empty by your late seventies. This doesn't mean it's gone. It just means you have paid income tax on it at a rate that is probably 10 to 15% less than the tax rate your children will pay on it. Another benefit to this strategy is this: if you leave investment assets to children and these assets have already had tax paid, your children will receive these assets income tax free. However, if an IRA is left to children as the sole death beneficiary, they will pay substantial income tax. If the estate will be subject to the Federal Estate Tax, and there is no plan in place, the IRA could lose more than 70% of its value to federal and state income tax as well as federal and state estate tax. Consult your legal planner to avoid this huge tax burden on the very assets you put away to enjoy during retirement.

A-B Tax Trust

Small business owners often find the A-B Tax Trust to be extremely helpful. It allows a husband and wife to preserve a $2 million inheritance for their heirs, tax free. If a couple does not implement an A-B Tax Trust, a 50% tax is levied upon assets over $1 million when the remaining spouse dies. This, of course, impacts the children, who are often the heirs.

YOU EARNED IT.

Ohio Estate Tax (a.k.a. state death tax)

You can calculate how the Ohio Estate Tax will affect you by subtracting $338,000 from your net estate and multiplying the difference by about 7%. However, if you gift in anticipation of death – within 36 months of dying – the state of Ohio will "recapture" the gifts to collect the tax. The gifts do not need to be returned; their values become part of the tax calculation. Again, planning now is prudent to your future as well as to the future of your heirs.

Federal (U.S.) Estate Tax (a.k.a. federal death tax)

Most small business owners develop their operations over many years, yielding a net asset value of the company at more than $1 million. Unless a complete plan is implemented (like an A-B Tax Trust mentioned earlier), the Federal (U.S.) Estate Tax will take 50% of everything over $1 million. Many times the second and third generation heirs will have to sell the company (or the farm) just to pay taxes. (Note the Death Tax is under change by Congress as of December 2004. The rate is 47% of assets exceeding $1.5 million.)

There are several ways to avoid the Federal Estate Tax.

Irrevocable Life Insurance Trust

If the small business owner is insurable, a life insurance policy can be purchased by the Trust to pay the taxes. But if the policy is owned by the insured, the money paid out at the insured's death goes into the estate and raises the taxes. A Trust keeps the life insurance policy out of the estate.

23

Limited Liability Company (LLC) or Family Limited Partnership

These are statutory entities that can own assets. Just like General Motors owns factories, your LLC can own properties. One big benefit is that the LLC acts as a shelter from creditors. No creditor of the company can reach your personal assets, and no personal creditor can attack your business assets. But the reason this can reduce the estate tax liability is because the assets may be given away to children or grandchildren at approximately a 30% discount (this factor varies according to the facts) for tax valuation when placed in the LLC.

LLC Example:

	VALUE	TAXABLE ESTATE	TAXES
FARM	$1,500,000 land	$500,000	$250,000
DEED INTO LLC	$1,000,000 30% discount	$0	$0

The shares of this LLC may be given to family members using the annual exclusion.

Charitable Remainder Trust (CRT)

This little-known legal device can turn hard assets, like buildings, into retirement income streams for life. Assets sold within the CRT will avoid capital gains taxes. Then at a certain date, the income (5 to 11% typically) will be generated for the donor for the rest of

YOU EARNED IT.

his or her life. This device can be very useful for seniors with rental properties who would rather have an IRA-like source of income. For example, a building or piece of real estate that has been appreciating for 20 to 40 years may be gifted into the CRT and sold with no tax consequences. This reduces your estate immediately by the value of the gifted asset (not 100%, but according to the IRA regulations), thereby reducing the estate tax liability. If the asset is sold, absolutely no capital gains taxes will be owed. That's because assets within a CRT live in a tax-free environment. Furthermore, income earned within the CRT is tax-free. And this CRT, of which you may be trustee, can be set up to provide a guaranteed income for your remaining life or the remaining years of both you and your spouse. This income stream is taxable as ordinary income or capital gains to the recipient. Additionally, you are allowed charitable tax deductions, which are usually limited to one-third of your gross income.

However, the very big negative associated with this device is that the road into the CRT is a one-way street. That asset will never go back into the estate. But, if this device will save you a 25% capital gains tax and save you a 50% federal estate tax, then leaving at least 10% of the original gift to charity (that's the IRS Rule) is not such a bad thing! After all, this is a tax-effective way to leave a legacy to your community.

To give you an idea of the power of this device, here is an example. Joan is a widow in her late sixties with an estate valued at $1.7 million. Throughout their married life, Joan and her husband worked hard and invested in properties. At his death, she owned all of the assets. In the 2002, the Federal Estate Tax required that any amount more than $1,000,000 would be taxed at 50%. That would have resulted in a potential Federal Estate Tax bill of $350,000 for Joan.

Joan decided she really didn't want to maintain the properties and wanted to sell them instead. These buildings had appreciated 10 times. Her original cost basis was only 10% of the current fair market value. If she sold the $1 million properties, she faced a capital gains tax of approximately $250,000. So her total tax bill for working hard and accumulating these assets would have been $600,000!

Joan created a CRT. Then she gifted the buildings into the trust, thus reducing her estate to $700,000, which became exempt under the 2002 Federal Estate Tax laws mentioned above. That saved her $350,000. Joan sold the buildings within the CRT, received $1 million for the sale, and paid no capital gains taxes at the time of sale. She saved $250,000! The CRT saved Joan and her family a total of $600,000! The best part is yet to come. Joan received a retirement income for her remaining years of about $100,000 per year – guaranteed! However, as mentioned earlier, this is taxable income. It may be deemed ordinary income or capital gains income depending on the management of the CRT.

CHAPTER 5

Step 5
CHOOSE NO PROBATE

There is no law that compels your estate to go through probate if you have implemented a plan that does not pass property – real or personal – through your Will. Your Will is a very important document, but you never want to rely on it to distribute personal or real property. A Will is an invitation to probate court!

Look at these comparisons:

	PROBATE	NO PROBATE
TIME	9 to 24 months	2 to 6 months
COST	3 to 10% of estate (average is 6%)	From a few hundred dollars to a few thousand, depending on the number of assets to be distributed
CONTEST	Beneficiary may or may not waive objections to estate, which can lead to a contest of Will	No waiver, or no notice necessary
REAL ESTATE	Real estate out of your home state would trigger an ancillary probate in the second jurisdiction	Valuations need to be done, then distribution of land in controlled legal Trust

To keep your estate distribution private and avoid probate, consider the following.

Gifting

We've already covered gifting in Chapter Four, but it applies here as well. Assets that you gift out of your estate will not be subject to probate. In addition, there is no waiting period when you gift an asset. But be careful, because there is a penalty period attached to gifting from the nursing home eligibility point of view and a 36-month gift recapture from an Ohio Estate Tax point of view.

YOU EARNED IT.

Beneficiary Documents

Financial devices like life insurance and annuities automatically avoid probate because beneficiaries are named on the policies. For securities accounts, a transfer-on-death letter can be executed. It will pass the account to the named beneficiaries on the letter without incurring probate. The same applies with payable-on-death letters for bank accounts and certificate of deposit (CD) accounts.

Use Life Estate Deeds or Transfer-on-Death Deeds to avoid probate on homes, farms, or vacation properties. If land is gifted, the donor's cost basis is gifted with it. That means the gift recipient (usually the children) will pay a large capital gains tax. By simply using a Life Estate Deed, the capital gains tax is eliminated.

Even though these assets avoid probate, they do not avoid estate taxes. Therefore, each of these assets must be accounted for when calculating the estate tax liability of the estate. However, from the date of death, the income generated on these accounts will become income for the named beneficiaries. That means there may not be an income tax liability for the estate. If there is a "death" or estate tax liability, and the beneficiaries already have the assets, where will the money come from to pay the taxes? This apportionment of the estate taxes is important to consider since the executor has the fiduciary duty to pay the taxes within nine months of death.

29

Joint Tenancy

This tool enables two people to own an asset. If both people named on the account own the asset outright, 100% of the asset is owned by the remaining owner when the first person dies. However, there is a dangerous aspect to joint tenancy. Here is an example: Dad has passed away and Mom is living alone but wants to visit her friends in Florida each winter. How does she take care of things while she's gone? Often, a son or daughter is named on Mom's account as joint tenant. This is convenient and will avoid probate. However, under banking laws, the child owns that account just as much as Mom does, so if the child is sued, Mom's account can be pursued to pay the debt or judgment against the child.

What's the answer? Simply put Mom's name only on Mom's account, and provide the child with a limited power or a general durable power of attorney to help Mom with the banking while she's out of town. This way the bank account does not belong to the child. Therefore any legal liability incurred by the child will not involve Mom's account.

Revocable Living Trust

This legal document holds assets owned by the trustee. It is extremely flexible because assets can be added with very little effort or cost. Every time a new asset is purchased, the Trust is named as the owner and the item is funded. "Funding the Trust" simply means re-titling assets in the name of the trustee of the Trust.

30

YOU EARNED IT.

Most people also appreciate the privacy involved with this Trust. It acts like a private Will but never has to be filed with the court. For example, a husband and wife create a Joint Revocable Living Trust. When the wife dies, there is little or no legal work to be done. The husband, now the remaining trustee, distributes any assets his wife had requested (like giving her engagement ring to her daughter) to be gifted. After the husband dies, the remaining assets are distributed according to the Trust.

All assets in a Revocable Living Trust are still subject to income taxation of the grantor and to nursing home spend-down. When families ask me to help them with nursing home planning, I sometimes have to revoke a Revocable Living Trust or take the assets out of the Trust in order to create an exempt status or to preserve them a different way.

Your Revocable Living Trust may not do what you want it to do if you don't keep it funded. For example, Joe Robbie owned the Miami Dolphins NFL football team and the stadium in which the team played. His estate plan included a Revocable Living Trust and a Pour Over Will. His Will was supposed to fund the Trust at the time of his death. After his death and before the assets could be funded into the Trust, his wife made a claim against the Will. She wanted to take her portion of the estate under Florida law. The estate has been in probate proceedings for many years and it still is not settled. The moral of the story is this: Fund your Revocable Living Trust and keep it funded during your lifetime to ensure those assets will avoid probate.

If you find yourself as the administrator, executor, executrix, or successor trustee of a loved one's estate that is in probate, understand that you are in control, not the attorney. You can even interview and choose the attorney to help you resolve the estate. Make sure you ask the following questions:

- What is the general process?

- How much of the work does the attorney do? How much can the executor do?

- What are the fees? How are they to be paid?

- How long is the process? Why?

If you are uncomfortable with any of the answers, interview another attorney. You will be working closely with the attorney, so you must trust him or her. To ensure you are well informed, here is an outline of the probate process if property is transferred through a Will:

- Collect original Will and certificate of death.

- Inventory all assets (date of death values).

- Inventory all liabilities.

- Establish an estate bank account to pay funeral bills, after appointing a fiduciary.

- Notify beneficiaries and creditors.

- A probate case must be opened at the county probate court. There are very specific forms for each county. Contact the county probate court to request them.

YOU EARNED IT.

- The next step depends on the levels of assets and the provisions of the Will dealing with real and personal property. Generally speaking, the estate must ensure the following are paid: funeral bill, estate taxes, and legal fees. The estate also is obligated to notify creditors. After these procedures have been followed, the final distribution is made to beneficiaries.

- If you are lucky, this process will take about a year. If there is a complication or contest, the process will take considerably more time.

If you are fortunate enough to be the executor of an estate where the assets avoid probate, the process is much simpler and shorter. Here is the probate-free process:

- Collect original Will and certificate of death.

- Inventory all assets titled to the decedent (date of death values).

- Inventory all liabilities and pay them.

- Determine and pay any taxes owed.

- Understand what the property distribution is from the decedent's Will/Trust documents.

- Obtain a file number from the county probate court only to file the estate tax.

- Distribute assets according to the wishes expressed by the deceased in his Will or Trust document.

This process should take 60 to 180 days.

CHAPTER 6

∾

Step 6
STOP NURSING HOME SPEND-DOWN

For most people, moving a family member into a nursing home is emotionally draining. It does not have to become a financial disaster as well! The September 2001 issue of the *Journal of Financial Planning* predicts that by 2010, 50% of the U.S. workforce will be involved with a nursing home while providing care for an elderly family member. This means that each American family

YOU EARNED IT.

needs to understand how nursing homes work and what their rights and obligations are.

In 2004, full-time nursing home care costs around $5,500 each month in Ohio. Additional medical costs can double that rate. Planning to protect assets from nursing home spend-down is just as necessary as a plan to reduce your income tax liability!

Medicare pays only 4 to 6% of nursing home bills. Consider this scenario: The average retired American senior lives on a pension and Social Security. Medicare kicks in at 65, and the senior also purchases a Medicare supplement policy. She thinks she has done everything "right."

If she becomes ill and undergoes cancer or heart surgery, Medicare and her supplemental insurance will most likely pay the bills. However, if she is diagnosed with Alzheimer's disease or has a stroke and needs long-term rehabilitation in a nursing home, Medicare will pay about 5% of her bills. That's because Medicare only pays for "skilled care" like surgery and not "intermediate care" or "custodial care" as she would receive in a nursing home.

With a proper plan, you can preserve your assets and your spouse's lifestyle if you need nursing home care. There are three ways to pay for nursing home care: insurance, your own income and assets, and publicly funded programs. More than 70% of nursing home residents are eligible for Medicaid payment of the nursing home bill. The federal/state funded Medicaid for nursing home reimbursement is the only long-term care strategy our government provides. There is no other discernable public strategy.

35

There are several common-sense methods to keep families out of poverty. Even with a family member in a nursing home, a competent elder law attorney may be able to save 50 to 60% of his or her assets. Usually, the residence or family business can be saved through proper planning, as well as about 50% of other assets like cash, CDs, and investments. The actual amounts vary depending on circumstances. One thing is for sure – the nursing home spend-down prevention plan is time-critical. The sooner you get started, the more effective the plan will be in saving assets!

First, let's focus on a few important rules regarding assets and income. To become eligible for Ohio's Medicaid program, which authorizes payment of home care or institutional care (nursing home), there are asset and income requirements:

- To qualify, the maximum asset level is $1,500. For couples, this only applies to the nursing home spouse. The community spouse can exempt the house (of any value), a car (of any value), and up to a maximum of $89,280 in other assets. The institutionalized spouse can only have $1,500 in the bank.

- There are exemption rules. The timing of the application and the determination of what's called the "snapshot date" are important in determining the ultimate amount of assets the community spouse can keep. For example, the difference in whether or not a family farm or home can be exempted is sometimes a matter of timing. Therefore, a sound plan must be formulated early in the process.

YOU EARNED IT.

- The community spouse retains his or her income. But what if the community spouse has no income? She may be a wife and mother who spent her lifetime raising the family and not working outside of the home. She obviously does not receive a pension and only a fraction of her husband's Social Security income. The good news is that her income can be augmented by the Minimum Monthly Maintenance Needs Allowance, which requests income back from the nursing home spouse.

- There are two periods of time to consider: the look-back period and the period of ineligibility. The look-back period is a period of 36 months from the date of application in which the Ohio Department of Job and Family Services (ODJFS) will inspect the applicant's financial history. ODJFS is trying to determine the level of assets and whether or not assets had been transferred for less than fair market value in anticipation of a nursing home stay. This look-back period changes to 60 months if assets have been transferred using a Trust. (In emergency planning, a Trust does not help you with nursing home planning.) The other period is called a "penalty period" or "period of ineligibility." This is never a fixed period of time. It is always calculated according to the value of the assets transferred during gifting. The formula: divide the asset value by the cost figure the ODJFS publishes as the Ohio Average Private Pay Rate of nursing home care per month ($4,512 per month in December 2004).

37

There is no law that forbids gifting. But each gift creates a period of ineligibility from receiving nursing home reimbursement.

Now let's look at some planning techniques. Of course, if planning is done during a time of good health and younger age, more options are available. Here are the planning techniques we will examine:

- Long-term care insurance

- Transferring real estate investments and cash assets (i.e., to a Family Trust)

- Emergency planning if your spouse or parent is already in a nursing home

- Keeping your home (not losing it to nursing home spend-down)

Long-term Care Insurance

This is a tool that can reduce or eliminate nursing home spend-down. However, it is most beneficial for young, healthy people in their fifties or sixties who can afford the premiums. Here are some questions you can ask your insurance provider to ensure he or she really understands the issues:

- How many seniors will need nursing home care? (About one in every two seniors by 2010.)

- What is the average length of stay in the nursing home? (87% of nursing home residents stay 36 months or less; 47% of residents stay 90 days or less; and 50% return home after rehabilitation.)

- How many policyholders make a claim against their policies?

YOU EARNED IT.

- How much will the premium decrease if we pay the nursing home bill for six months? (Should be about a 25 to 30% reduction.) You will also learn that the "elimination period" or "waiting period" is really your deductible (i.e., you pay the nursing home bill during this time).

- Are the premiums tax deductible?

- Do I continue to pay the premiums if I'm in the nursing home? Is there any way to get value from the policy even if I don't have a nursing home stay?

- Can the premiums be returned to me after so many years?

- Is there a life insurance type policy that has a long-term care rider on it? (The answer is yes.)

- Can the insurance company raise the premiums at any time? What is the record of the insurance company you are considering with respect to raising premiums?

- Does the policy cover nursing home-type expenses for care in my home, like building costs associated with enlarging doors and installing ramps if I'm in a wheelchair?

- Does the policy cover assisted-living facility care? Or even hospice care? Do I get to choose the facility?

Although there are a lot of questions to consider about this type of insurance, you should still consider it. If you have a pre-existing condition like cancer, diabetes, heart attack, stroke, Parkinson's disease, dementia or Alzheimer's disease, you most likely will be denied coverage or at least be "rated" for a higher premium. Remember that insurance companies are in business to make money. They usually win financially on their "bets" with clients. However, long-term care insurance really works for some people. Here are some parameters to keep in mind when selecting long-term care insurance:

- **How long should you buy it?**
  I recommend no more than 36 to 48 months. Statistically, 87% of nursing home residents are out in less than 36 months. And if you have 36 months covered with insurance, then all of your assets, which would ordinarily be in jeopardy of spend-down, can be saved.

- **How much should you buy?**
  The average nursing home bill per month in 2002 was $3,903, or $130 per day. Remember, you still have income and some assets to support the payment, so I recommend about 75 to 80% coverage. That means about $100 per day. If there is 15 to 20 years between your current age and your 80th birthday, then get the inflation rider as well.

- **When will the insurance begin paying?**
  The shorter the elimination period, the higher the premium. Standard policies range from 20 to 90 days. If you want to lower your premium and already have an asset base to support you, then ask for a 120 to 180 day elimination period. I call this "the catastrophic approach." If you need rehabilitation in a nursing home for a few

months, you are committed to paying the bill. But if catastrophe strikes, such as a paralyzing accident, a stroke, or Alzheimer's disease or Parkinson's disease, your stay will be beyond six months, and you will have insurance to pay the bill.

Transfer of Assets

If you don't want insurance, and you have every reason to believe that you will remain healthy for some years, then you might consider transferring assets into a Life Estate Deed (for real estate assets), a Safe Fund (for cash assets), a Family Trust, a Family Limited Partnership, or a Family Corporation.

If you fear you or your wife might eventually enter a nursing home, you can create a Life Estate Deed that gives your heirs the remainder (or future) interest in the home. This gives the community spouse (the spouse not in the nursing home) the right to live there until death. This not only avoids probate, but also saves the house from being sold to pay the nursing home bill after the period of ineligibility has expired. You don't want to gift the house to your child because you suffer maximum penalty periods, you lose control, and the children pay the capital gains taxes.

The "rule of halves" preserves cash assets from nursing home spend-down. A senior can gift half of his or her cash to a child, who puts it into a Safe Fund, which could be a Family Trust started by the child. That Safe Fund preserves the assets that the family may

41

Example of Gifting a House:

$$\text{Applicant's number of ineligible months} = \frac{\text{Auditor's value of house} \quad X \quad \text{CMS factor (based on applicant's age)}}{\$4{,}512}$$

Auditor's Value of House: $100,000
Applicant's Age: 75 years old

$$\frac{\$100{,}000 \ X \ \text{CMS FACTOR} \ \textit{(BASED ON AGE)}}{\$4{,}512}$$

= 10 MONTHS OF INELIGIBILITY

need in the future. The only negative aspect is that the gift creates a period of ineligibility, which means you can't apply for assistance during this penalty period. Therefore, an elder law attorney will conduct an analysis to allow enough remaining assets to pay for the senior's care during the penalty period. However, if you create this Safe Fund early enough in your life, the penalty period will be less of an issue.

A Family Trust is another way to protect assets from nursing home spend-down. It is usually an Irrevocable Trust, which is funded with assets that will be available for the family members who are the lifetime beneficiaries. The assets are protected once they are in the Trust. If the Trust is constructed properly, the trustee, who can be different from the grantor, will have

YOU EARNED IT.

absolute discretion for distribution of assets and income from the Trust. The Trust has its own tax ID number, and income tax returns must be filed each year.

The Family Trust is an excellent method for heirs to employ to protect assets that really are "early bequests" from creditors of the heirs. The income and assets can be used for any purpose the trustee deems necessary for family harmony. This Trust also has its own tax number, and the trustee will file a tax return each year. As long as income to the Trust is distributed to the beneficiaries, the beneficiaries will pay tax at their income tax rate.

Emergency Planning

In a situation where an individual is already in a nursing home or is about to enter one, an emergency plan can be designed to prevent impoverishment. It will not prevent spend-down, but it will prevent spending down everything!

Let's look at a couple with $250,000 in assets. This includes a house worth $80,000 and bank assets of $170,000. If the husband goes into a nursing home, the division of assets rule will allow the house to be exempt if the wife remains in it. In addition, one car is exempt as well as half of the bank assets. That means $85,000 is in jeopardy.

There's really only one way to save that money – gift the assets out of the estate. If these assets had been in an Irrevocable Trust for at least 60 months, they would have been protected and not available under the law for spend-down. Assuming those techniques were not used, we would gift out of the estate.

43

Remember, every time there is a gift, there is a resulting penalty period. During that period, there must be enough money to allow private payment of nursing home fees. For example, if the pension income of the nursing home spouse is $1,000, and the nursing home bill is $4,000 per month, there must be at least $3,000 per month available for every penalty month incurred.

Also remember that for every $3,903 gifted (APPR), there is a one-month penalty period. So if $45,000 was gifted, the penalty period would be 11 months, and the spend-down would be about $33,000. After the penalty period, the nursing home spouse would be eligible for public benefits under Medicaid to pay subsequent nursing home bills as long as the asset base is $1,500 or below. This type of emergency planning is called an Estate Split Plan. A line in the sand is drawn that defines the limit of the family spend-down. Instead of spending down to nothing, this strategy allows the burden to be shared. Without doing this, the community spouse will be "sentenced" to impoverishment for the rest of his or her retirement.

Let's turn our attention to gifting. When the $45,000 is gifted out of the estate, usually a child or sibling assists with the transaction. That child can set up a Family Trust or other financial vehicle to make sure that the gifted money will be insulated from the liabilities of the donor. This is really important because the gifted money is the only resource left for the nursing home spouse, and it must complement the resources available for the community spouse to maintain his or her standard of living. Often, this gifting strategy allows the community spouse to remain in the house and not be forced to sell the house just to have income.

YOU EARNED IT.

Summary

Everyone must be aware of high nursing home costs and the financial hardships that can result. Even though only about one-third of the senior population is affected, none of us knows the future, so planning is prudent.

If assets are transferred to an Irrevocable Trust, seniors won't be protected for 60 months. Therefore, if long-term care insurance is possible, the insured should keep it in effect to get through the 60-month period of ineligibility.

If insurance is not possible, this 60-month look back period is too expensive to risk. Therefore, the Estate Split Plan or advanced gifting strategy may be more appropriate.

The usual look-back period is 36 months. Gifting during that period must be reported to the Ohio Department of Jobs and Family Services. Many Department officials will instruct the applicant to return the gift. This is not required by law! As long as the period of ineligibility is over, there is no negative impact from gifting.

Since nursing home rules are different in each state, please consult a Certified Elder Law Attorney (CELA) in your state. Go to www.NAELA.com to find an attorney in your area.

Let me describe one case where planning saved a business. A couple had run a family contracting business for more than 40 years. When the wife became ill and needed nursing home assistance, neither the Ohio Department of Job and Family Services, nor his

45

attorneys, or financial advisors told the husband that his business (income-producing property) was exempt from spend-down. He and I worked together to allocate the proper assets to the business, thereby alleviating spend-down. In fact, had we not worked together, the husband would have liquidated the business just to pay the nursing home bill. Not only did the proper plan stop the spend-down, but it also saved the business for their children.

The vast majority of seniors face financial disaster if either spouse requires a nursing home stay. Families must put a plan in place to avoid financial ruin.

CHAPTER 7

Step 7
REGULAR REVIEW

Review your plan regularly. Your life is dynamic, things change, and so should your plan.

Laws change, your mind may change, or your family relationships may change. Therefore, you need a common sense plan that is flexible enough to accommodate these changes and won't cost you a bundle each time a change is necessary.

Regular review is necessary, and reviewing your plan is as important as having a plan. Take advantage of planned reviews at regular intervals. It is a lot easier and less expensive to plan for change than to deal with it on an emergency basis.

Every two to three years should be sufficient for review. But if a significant medical, financial, or family event occurs, a review may be warranted to determine if additional liability has been exposed.

CHAPTER 8

❧

SMALL BUSINESS

Most family businesses conduct business as sole proprietorships. Farmers, dry cleaners, store owners, electricians, and plumbers generally do not want the perceived complexity of a business entity – that is, tax returns and filing. However, both state and federal laws favor business entities with tax benefits. Issues like taxation, creditor protection, and passing family wealth to the next generation can all be enhanced through some form of business entity. In this chapter, you will read about business entities and their benefits.

Family Limited Partnership or Limited Liability Company (LLC)

The Family Limited Partnership is slowly being replaced by the Limited Liability Company simply because no member of the LLC has unlimited liability.

The LLC is a statutory business entity that allows several people to do business in a protected way. The members of the LLC can be divided into voting members and non-voting members. Each member contributes assets to the LLC. Generally, LLCs are established to protect assets of the LLC from being attacked by creditors of individual members.

For example, if a member is involved in an auto accident and is found to be liable, a judgment cannot easily be levied against the LLC assets. People who have a judgment against a member can be prevented from attaching the debt to that member's assets in the LLC.

The LLC can conduct business using the concepts of the corporation, but the profits or losses "flow-through" to the members. Therefore, the double taxation of a normal corporation is avoided.

Along with the creditor protections, another key benefit is the ability to reduce the valuation of one's assets. Since this is a private company, the IRS allows certain discounts for "lack of marketability" and for any "minority interest." This discounting schedule is complicated and you certainly must consult an attorney or CPA, but generally the IRS allows a discount of 20 to 30%. For example, this reduces a $1.5 million property to about $1.0 million valuation and avoids a $250,000 Federal Estate Tax liability.

YOU EARNED IT.

In summary, many family businesses conduct operations under an LLC because of the valuation advantages and creditor protection attributes.

Special Needs Trusts (SNT)

If you have a disabled child or beneficiary, and you wish to leave an inheritance to him or her, do not leave it to the child. Leave it to a Special Needs Trust. With the assets in an SNT, the disabled child will still be eligible for Supplemental Security Income or Medicaid. This can make a big difference in a disabled person's quality of life.

Summary

Seniors must develop a retirement plan that takes into consideration a possible nursing home stay or an expensive treatment at home. The easy answer – but most expensive usually – is to obtain long-term care insurance.

However, for those many seniors who can't afford the premiums or can't get the coverage because of pre-existing illnesses, you are still able to execute a plan to prevent impoverishment.

Just like tax planning and probate avoidance planning, nursing home spend-down planning is critical to your peace of mind. With the recent estate tax changes, both federal and state, death taxes are not of paramount importance. Medical costs, pharmaceutical bills, nursing home or assisted living costs are now the biggest financial risk you will have in senior years.

There are ways to prevent or minimize taxes and nursing home spend-down, but seniors have the task of finding advisors whom they trust implicitly. No longer can we count on the government to advise us of what would be in our own best interest. Each of us needs to learn these laws, ask questions of our advisors, and develop a plan to preserve assets we have so diligently worked for during our lives.

Good luck and good planning!

Definition of Terms

Last Will and Testament: This is a vital and essential document every person should have. It spells out who will handle the estate and how assets will be distributed. Since your family situation may change and since tax laws and estate laws can also change, it is important to review your Will every five years.

Pour Over Will: This is a Last Will and Testament, but it specifically "pours" all assets left in the decedent's estate into an existing trust that had been established prior to death. The Pour Over Will should only be used as a last resort because it requires a probate proceeding.

Durable Power of Attorney for finance and legal matters: In order to execute this document properly, it must provide specific financial instructions with regard to bank accounts, investment accounts, insurance companies, real estate transactions, trusts, gifting, and nomination of a guardian.

Health Care Power of Attorney: The person making this document gives another individual power for making his or her health care decisions when he or she is unable to do so.

Living Will: This is a sister document to the Health Care Power of Attorney. The Living Will is used in a very narrow scope. When the maker of the document is in a terminal condition, the Living Will tells medical professionals whether he or she wishes to be put on life support.

HIPAA: Federal Privacy Act which must be waived to allow your representative to access your medical files.

Trusts: Broadly defined, these legal documents help position assets to solve specific legal problems.

Living Revocable Trust: This is a Trust very commonly used to avoid probate. It must be funded before it is effective. It does nothing more than ensure assets avoid probate.

Irrevocable Family Trust: The assets that are assigned into the Trust will never come back out of that Trust to the donor. Essentially, the assets are on "hold" until you pass away; therefore, people use this type of Trust sparingly because the donor loses control over the enjoyment of the assets. There is one benefit, though. If you own real estate that has appreciated greatly, you can place it the Irrevocable Family Trust for your children upon your death. This way you keep the appreciation out of your estate, thereby lowering taxes.

Special Needs Trust that is Self-Settled: Disabled individuals set up this Trust to protect themselves from "spending-down" all their finances to qualify for Medicaid reimbursement. However, this Trust must contain a payback provision to Medicaid.

Special Needs Trust (established by a third party): A parent, guardian, or spouse of a disabled person sets up this Trust. The assets within the Trust do not belong to the disabled individual, therefore no payback provision to Medicaid is required.

YOU EARNED IT.

Family Dynasty Trust: This Trust is irrevocable at the death of the grantor. The assets within the trust are never distributed out of Trust; they are held in the Trust for the beneficiaries. In other words, the Trust goes on forever. For example, you can place $1 million into a Family Dynasty Trust for your future generations. Your children will benefit from the interest during their lifetimes, but they can never touch the $1 million. When your children die, their children benefit from the interest during their lifetimes, and so on. Think of "dynasty" as "multi-generational."

Charitable Remainder Trust: There are many benefits to this Trust:

- When assets within this Trust are sold, there may be no capital gains taxes.
- If the assets earn income, there may be no income tax.
- When the donor of the Trust provides a gift from the Trust to an individual, the donor may receive a charitable tax credit.
- This Trust can also provide income for the donor, whether it be for five, 10, or 15 years, or even lifelong. If the donor dies during this time, the remainder of the income goes to the donor's beneficiaries. But there may be estate tax consequences when income is left to heirs.
- The Trust allows for a legacy to be left to a charitable organization. If the assets are sufficient, a Family Foundation can be established. The donor's heirs manage the foundation to ensure that the charitable intent of the donor is carried out.

55

Institutionalized Spouse: This is a term used on nursing home applications. It simply refers to the spouse going into the nursing home.

Community Spouse: This is the spouse living outside of the nursing home.

Ohio Estate Recovery Tax: This tax allows the Attorney General's office to collect back from the decedent's estate any monies that were paid by the state to a nursing home.

Look-Back Period: This is a period of inspection "looking back" from the date of application for Medicaid. The applicant's financial history is reviewed to see if any gifts or transfer of assets occurred. The look-back period is usually 36 months.

Period of Ineligibility: The period of ineligibility is calculated specifically for each gift made. It is calculated by dividing the amount of the gift by the average private pay rate (see below) in Ohio.

Average Private Pay Rate: The average rate paid each month for a room in a nursing home in Ohio. ($3,903 in August, 2002)

Ohio Department of Jobs and Family Services: This state department is responsible for deciding Medicaid eligibility.

If you would like more information about estate planning and asset preservation, contact Don at:

www.chapinlawoffices.com